UPRISING
An Evolution into
Womanhood and Self-Discovery

TASHA CAMERON

Copyright © 2021 Tasha Cameron

All rights reserved. No part of this book may be reproduced or used in any manner without the prior written permission of the copyright owner, except for the use of brief quotations in a book review.

To request permissions,
contact the publisher at cupofsweettee.com.

Paperback: 978-1-7372344-0-1
Ebook: 978-1- 7372344-1-8

First paperback edition September 2021.

Cover & Interior Art by Calvin Keith Rose II

cupofsweettee.com
Facebook: Cup Of Sweet Tee
Instagram: sweettee52

DEDICATIONS

The Cameron's

To my mother Ruby Jewel

who raised a strong, independent woman. She always said leading by example was the greatest teacher, and that was her greatest gift to me.

To my brother Edward James

The unconditional love you gave to me was like no other. It was you and I until the end.

You are tremendously missed.

CONTENTS

Dedications iii

Introduction vii

Part I: Embody 1

Part II: Belong 37

Part III: Evolve(d) 71

Success 109

Acknowledgements 111

Uprising
Noun
An act of rising up; an ascent or activity.
Verb
To come into existence or prominence; to come above the horizon.

Uprising is my poetic take on life. It's about wandering in the wilderness and wondering what this life has to offer. It's about taking off the blinders that we recognize as normalcy and digging deep to find our truths. It's about battling our minds into staying the course, while searching for a freedom that satisfies the mind, body and soul.

From the time that we were born, we were taught to be prim and proper. "Girls don't do this," and "a young lady never does that." We were molded into what our parents and society thought and said we should be and should become.

We are emotional, nurturers, always eager and wanting to please rather than be pleased and appease ourselves. We are being bombarded into thinking that the only things that matter are our emotional statuses and the worldly possessions we have or have yet to acquire...our

ASS-ets, but not anymore!

Women are evolving. There is an uprising amongst us. It's the ongoing struggle to blaze our own trails and to succeed on levels that our foremothers never dared.

I had written these poems many years ago with no idea of how I was going to use them. As I dug deeper into my own spirituality, it occurred to me that a lot of my poetry may shed some light onto a journey that others may be embarking on.

I still continue to have bumps in the road on my own Journey, to a freedom unbound. I am learning that I am more than enough, that I have what it takes to see this thing through, and I'm here to let you know that you are enough and you do too!

This collection of poems is broken down into three parts, in a way that I hope all women can relate to.

PART I: EMBODY

Embody

Verb (used with subject)

To give a concrete form to; express, personify or exemplify in concrete form.

To collect into or include in a body; organize, incorporate.

To embrace or comprise

    It's sex appeal, becoming of age, finding love, falling in love, hurting because of love. All of these things women have embodied in their lifetime.

    It's just like us (women), to explore and emotionalize everything we come in contact with, and then take that with which we have connected and make it personal. By trying to fix it, mold it and incorporate it into something we want or something we think we must have. Organizing it, so that it makes sense to us and to what society says we have inherited.

    So, it begins…

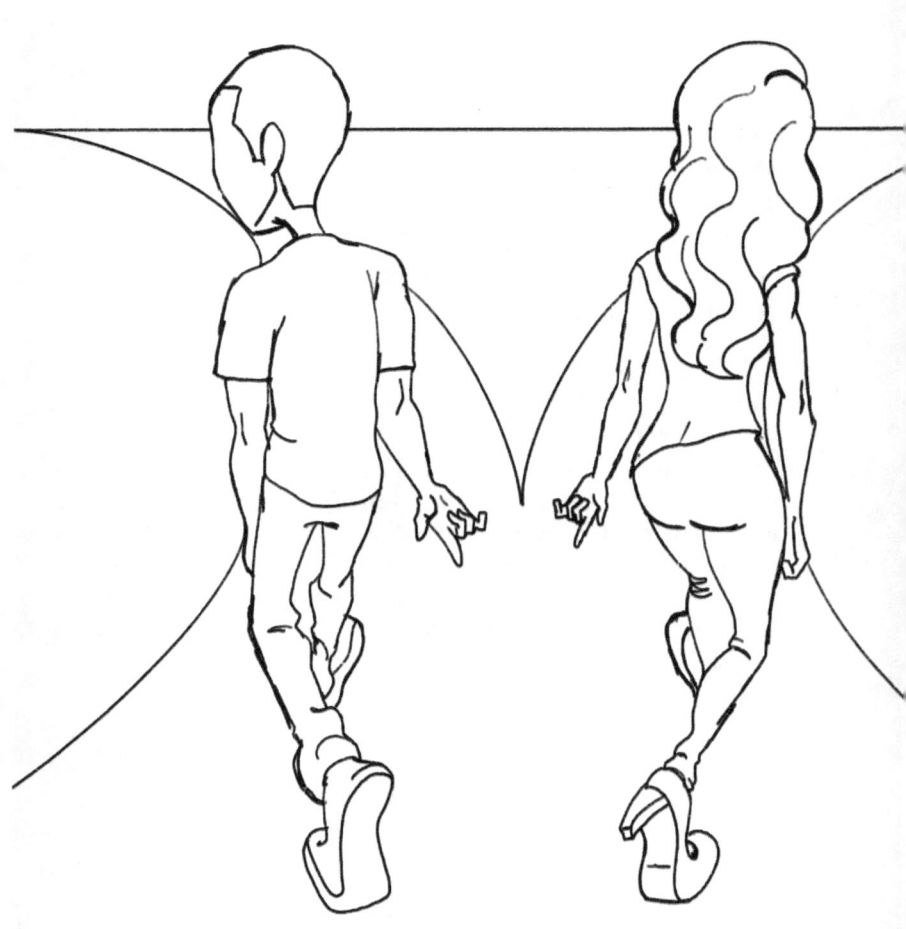

JOURNEY I

They traveled together for many years
The silence was deafening
Neither knew where they were going
They just knew they were being call upon
Called upon…Why?
Each silently asked themselves
For none had the answer
They would have to wait and see
Their travels took them over many mountains
Through many valleys, too
Obstacles stood in the way sometimes, but the calling still came and still they followed
What seems like decades of searching and coming up with nothing finally made sense
The calling was from within and to be answered by themselves for themselves
The journey of life is never easy and one that is made alone
"They" was their first mistake

PLAYER

Your late-night rendezvous elude me not one bit
Your explanations of whereabouts
What, you think that they're legit?
Don't play yourself or better yet don't try to play me
You think that I'm so stupid that I can't even see
See your lies, see your games
See my love burn down in flames
Just like the hold you had on me
You got your wish, I'll let you be
To sprout my wings and learn to fly
No more questions or wondering why
No regrets and no mistakes
Best of all, no more heartache

HEAT

In the heat of passion, psychotic, erotic
The rhythm we have flows like a river
A boat perhaps rocking and swaying
As underneath you I am laying
The gentle groans in which I hear
The purr-like moans I whisper in your ear
Then in an instant orgasms explode
My legs shaking while your pistol unloads
With gentle hands you caress my face
As we hold each other in a warm embrace

LOST

In a field of dreams is where you left my heart

My instincts told me not to go, but falling in love is exactly what I did do.

I thought there were no secrets between me and you

A sheltered life is what I led

Until you showed me the world

Made me feel special, told me I was unique and that I would always be your girl

In wide-open spaces with unfamiliar faces, you lead my heart astray. While loneliness took over

as visions of you slowly faded away.

In this field of dreams and spaces, my self-esteem faltered to an all-time low

After some time realizing you were never mine, probably right from the start

It was time for me to move on

Trying hard to be strong

You became a memory in my mind

SURRENDER

In the midst of my confusion, you were the only sane thing I could think of
All thoughts of you made sense
I relaxed and my nerves became settled you are good for me
In my heart I know this but the feelings aren't following through
When the good things come upon us we are blind to them
The things we do not need we long for
How can I surrender myself to you
When I cannot even acknowledge the state in which I evolve in myself

YOU SAID

You Said you'd never leave
Then walked out without a care
Never mind the hurt you caused
The pain, anguish and despair
You said you'd be my shelter
My wall, my rock, my saint
But when it came right down to it
You were only a thin layer of paint
You said for my eyes only
Then blank stares were all you gave
The darkness was too cold to bare
For my sunshine soul to save
You said you gave me the best
To which I'd have to disagree
If that was true my darling
Then you best would have set me free

BETWEEN THE TWO

Was I right to stay and lead you on
Knowing my feelings have been long gone
Having decided that I was fed up
Taking a lover because I didn't give a fuck
He was my lover, I was your wife
He was my lover and I was your wife
It was a fine line but I walked the two
One had what I wanted, the other not a clue
I knew one day I would have to choose
And knew exactly who would be the one to lose
But still I went closer, closer to the edge
Pushed every button, took advantage
He was my lover, I was your wife
It turned out in the end that I was all wrong
I was the loser all along
He was my lover, I was your wife
He WAS my lover and I WAS your wife

SO LONG AGO

Feeling you
Feeling me
Feelings we
Should have shared so long ago
As if time stood still
Telling you
Telling me
Telling us
To trust
What we see in our minds is real
And our hearts seal
Bond together as one
Time stands still for no man or wo-man
Time lost is time wasted
Wasted in haste of our denying our love for so long
Above all
To ourselves
Honestly you
Honestly me
Honestly we
Should have let it go a long time ago

EMOTIONS OF INSANITY

It was the loneliness that made me long for you

It was the bitterness that made me hate you

It was the emptiness that made me want you

Regardless of a whole string of emotions that were absent but present at the same time

Confusing me and blinding me but feeding me and nourishing me

My soul was lost and my mind was shut down

My heart was bleeding for your attention

Instead what I received was heartache and a broken spirit and bouts with insanity

But this was not my intention

It was my intention to be strong and hold on for the duration

It was my intention to try and change what you have become

Knowing full well that it was an impossible dream of make-believe

Because in the real world shit don't happen that way and still I held on tight

Tighter than I realized

Tighter than I should have

So tight that when you drew your last breath I still

Held on tightly to you neck

A NIGGA LIKE YOU

A nigga like you
Will make a sista forget herself; nose opened wide
A nigga like you
Will make a sista lose sight of everything; her pride
A nigga like you
Breaks a sister's spirit; hopes and dreams
A nigga like you
Won't let her be a queen
A nigga like you
Can't be her king
A nigga like you
Busy doin' his own thing
Can't see past himself, let alone see me
A nigga like you
Will never let things be
Cause a nigga like you
Can't see the reality of me being free

CARDS ON THE TABLE

Is it me you love or is it the sex? Straight up
Nose wide open I can see through to your brain
How you say I stroke you is just insane
Can it be that good or am I just misunderstanding
As to all these feelings that we have been commanding
We've become involved much to our dismay
Things were not supposed to happen this way
As time goes by and the hours turn to days
Days turn into months and those months have become years
We are still holding onto our fears
Such a tight grip I've had on you
Missing you in fear of losing you
Something that was never really mine
You know it is only a matter of time
That all things will be revealed and only then
Will our love be sealed
When you are able to set her free
with no regrets, and no upsets
Then the cards will be flat out on the table

DICKMATIZED

I was hypnotized, mesmerized
At a loss for all words
At a standstill, in a zone
Struck to the core of my bone
How it looked to me, looked at me
Fully erect and at attention
Remembering how I wanted it so bad
Dickmatized.... Did I mention?
Panting, heaving and receiving
Glowing from within
The things that we did
Shit.... It was a sin!
Dickmatized, yeah, I said it
So now the truth has come out
Has me swooning, crooning damn near drooling just thinking about
I can't even lie my ass was sprung
10 inches and to the left that damn thing hung
Beating on my ass like a big bass drum
Cum baby cum baby cum
And I have to be honest
That when it was all said and done
It was true that on his every word I hung
Shit.... It wasn't his love that I craved for
I was dickmatized dammit, need I say more!

LOVE JONES

Beads of sweat trickle down my face
An addict of love this jones I chase
Convulsions of feelings
These shakes I can't hide
Feeling like this and still be alive
Man you've got a hold on me
Been praying to God that you'd set me free
Remembering the feelings that we once shared
How I believed that you really cared
How you drained the blood from my veins
Telling my mind my actions weren't insane
My brother, My lover
My pusher, My friend
Relentless to succumb to that love jones again

FIRST AND LAST

First thoughts
First ideas
First words
First impressions
First love
You and I
The first to be the last
The race to finish first
In your arms I will always first love you
And last to leave
The first kisses we shared
Here in my life you are first and last

EXHALE

As I turned and watched him walk away tears came to my eyes
Like the rain falling from the clouds way up high
Knowing it wasn't meant to be
Although love hurt and blinded me
I refused to believe that I had failed
The ship has gone, the boat has sailed
I exhaled….
Losing you was harder than I imagined
Getting over you was even worse
How do I find the love I thirst?
Visions of you stayed on my mind
Thinking why has love treated me so unkind?
Another love like you was hard to find
I exhaled….
Coming to grips with what went on
Now finding solutions so I can stay strong
The inevitable has happened
I'm free from loves grip
I exhaled a deep breath as I've
Relinquished it

YOUNG LOVE

She was sixteen, he was thirty-two
The love they shared she felt was true
Too young for love all her friends said
Paid no attention to what her parents forbid
She said he made her life complete
That others were jealous and full of conceit
They all told her that she was a fool
Love was betrayal, deceitful and cruel
She has her whole life to live
At age sixteen she was only a kid
He got what he wanted, he talked a good game
In the end you were left feeling alone and ashamed

DREAMER

Two lives binding together as one
Embrace each other in the heat of the sun
Lying there together as the beach meets the sea
Looking in each other's eyes, could this be me?
I've longed for someone to completely understand how I feel
Now you've come along, can this actually be real?
We talked and we laughed and had such a good time
Actually got to know each other and things seemed just fine
The perfect relationship seemed to good to be true
Then I looked in the mirror and realized…I was dreaming about you.

FORGET ME NOT

Crimson colored sunsets
Across a crystal sky
Images surround me
Sounds are fluttering by
Visions of the moonlight
Stars dancing way up high
The feelings of belonging
You were here by my side
As light shines through an open window
Heat from the sun warms my face
As I'm remembering your smile
The touch of your embrace
Looking out over the hills
As their greenness turns to blue
The air flows flawlessly reminding me of you
Unlike the butterfly whose path of flight is free
You had your own life to live
I had to let you be
As I'm hoping you're smiling
When you're remembering me

LOVE STAGES

It's been a long time since I've washed any man's clothes
Allow him the key to my castle, let alone a seat on my throne
I've had a few visitors from time to time
Never anything lasting or worthy of calling him mine, and then here came you
From right outta the blue
Have me cooking and cleaning, wanting and believing unto my own self that love can be true Wondering, if the same can be said about you?
You not wanting to rush but taking your time, it seemed as though that was your favorite line
I like how you showed me patience and how you claimed I wore you thin
Those were the beginnings of our relationship back then
As time pushed on you wore on me too…
These were the beginning stages of how I've come to love you.

AGE AIN'T NOTHING BUT A NUMBER

No one understands the way we feel
The intense emotions are all too real
To push aside and try to hide
To let you go is suicide
Age ain't nothin' but a number
They could never appreciate the love that we share
This is from the heart not a one-night affair
But they don't care if we say it ain't fair
Age ain't nothin' but a number
Do I dare, no baby I swear
I ain't goin' nowhere
The true test is time, and they will find that
Age ain't nothin' but a number

LOVE SNEAK UP ON ME

To my surprise before my eyes
love came up and found me
I did not search or peer or prod
Not even a prayer was said to my God
yet somehow it still was there
gently letting me know that it cared
In different forms it came and went
not one time did it resent
When I turned my back away and frowned
Just stood there firm on solid ground
My husband, my sons are the forms love found
Through this love my life's turned around

TEARING STARS OF REMEMBRANCE

Just a glimpse of your reflection told me how long it's been since my heart has missed you

A fallen tear of remembrance brings to mind all the things we used to share

When together we discovered each other under blue black skies decorated with bright stars that seemed so close, that we could reach right up and grab them.

Holding each other close as if at any moment things would unravel and become undone and

just like that you were gone from my grasp

Under the blue black sky with bright stars so close, close enough to reach right up and grab them.

The air seemed to seep out of my lungs. Breaths so thick like smoke, my life had crashed and

Burned

The touch of your closeness is for what I yearned for

Unraveled and undone, I had to move on

The tears of remembrance soon became tears of joy and a glimpse of your reflection told

me how long it's been since my heart has grown strong, even without you.

A REBELS LOVE

Like a tall drink of water
You quenched my thirst
In my quest for love
You were my first
Every endeavor that I've ever tried
You were right there by my side
Never a disagreement or bit of restraint
Knowing that you had not a thing to gain
You helped me through the roughest of times
And still you seemed not to mind
A rebel at heart, with a gentle soul
Our rebel love story won't go untold

36 AND COUNTING

There was a time in my life
When I tried to please everyone
Everyone except for me
Now at 36 years of age I've finally
Made up my mind to concentrate on me
No matter what that might be
I'm finally satisfied with myself
My looks, my attitude (although no one's perfect), my job, my weight (although I would like to
tone up)
I'm satisfied and just maintaining
I've been seeing things through new glasses
Looking out for me
It may not be agreeable for others, but I need to find myself and love myself no matter who it
may hurt
Maybe it seems selfish, but I need to grow and become comfortable with myself and my
sexuality
These are the perceptions of me

ODE TO LUST

Big butt; thick thighs
Damn those pretty brown eyes
Slim waist; big bust
Makes a Nigga lust
That smile; those hips
Such thick kissable lips
Deep dimples; long hair
Man, it just ain't fair
Looking in the mirror I ask…
Is this all of what they see?
The beauty that is only skin deep
And not the inner working of me
To play the game fairly, you may as well not play it at all
To think that love will save you
Keep the quarter from making that call
It's all one big illusion
A designed state of confusion
To keep a sista guessing
Meanwhile a brutha keeps on pressing
His dick all up in another chick's space

YELLOW COLORED LOVE

It was yellow

That is the color that comes to mind when I hear your name being mentioned

Memories of you flood my senses

My heart begins to race anticipating the thought of your return

Then I realize you are gone, you're not coming back to me

It was agreed between the two of us that the differences were just too great

Time apart was what you said, needed time to clear your head

While all along you had moved on to greener pastures

Was I that blind?

Unclear, love had made me lose focus I forgot about me in the process

My life I had put on hold, trying to be everything and everybody you wanted me to be

How silly of me to think that I could ever change the way things had grown to be

When in reality you have forgotten me

It was yellow

That was the color that comes to mind when I hear your name being mentioned.

WASTED LOVE

As many times my thoughts of you have distracted the task at hand

Some things that have taken place I will never come to fully understand

Feeling as if time has stood still and the only thing keeping track was my heart

Knowing that loving you was wrong from the start

Who was I to resist your charm

Your extended hand in the crook of my arm

Whispering softly in my ear

The words that I so desperately wanted to hear

The need to be needed

The anguish of wanting what could never be mine

Holding onto a love that is obviously blind

And seemingly such a waste of time

STANDING BY

Even when the light shines bright
I still feel the reins of darkness
Holding tightly onto me as if it were
Choking the breaths of air right out of my lungs
I tried to exhale away the pain
But with each inhale it expands to new heights
And my heart sinks ever so slowly
To where I'm afraid that I won't be able to retrieve it
Like dry rotted cloth I'm falling apart at the seams
Trying to get you to hold on to your dreams
Keep hope alive, keep your head up when you stride
Although right now things are on the downside
Raising you was hard, but I did the best I could do
The love I have in my heart will never let me give up on you…
Roses do grow from concrete
And a mother's love is just that strong

IN THE MIDST

In the midst of my emotions
It seemed that time stood still
Alerting me to my defenses, and to my weaknesses
What I see when I look at you
Is the sincereness in your eyes
What I feel when I'm around you
Is the calmness in your voice
How your relaxing smile
Entices me to be more open
To refrain from my inhibitions
To be free, to feel free to explore me
In the midst of everything in this crazy world
I found you

OPEN WINDOW

Open window, breeze blowing through my hair
As I sit and stare
Watching, gazing, remembering you there
Just across the courtyard, how our eyes met
How you made me forget
The days, the ways, the changes
Any way the wind blows it takes my breath away
My heart skips a beat
The feeling of deceit makes me feel ashamed
And I look away
Realizing that you are not there
The courtyard is bare
A fragment of my imagination
As I sit and stare
Open window, breeze blowing through my hair

PART II: BELONG

Belong
Verb (used without object)

To be in the relation of a member, adherent, inhabitant.

To have the proper qualifications; especially socially.

To be proper or due, be properly or appropriately placed, situated.

As women we are constantly trying to navigate the ins and outs, the ups and downs, and yes, even sometimes finding ourselves sliding sideways.

It's when finding our place becomes filling that hole in our souls, that we all are on a mission to do. It's standing up and standing tall when society measures everything according to how powerful it is or by how wealthy it is.

Everyone's a critic, quick to criticize and pass judgement. It's learning not to keep up with Joneses' in a rat race full of folks who are only looking just to find more cheese. It's about finding OUR cheese and learning to be okay with standing alone! The cheese stands alone, so it continues…

WHO STOLE MY CHEESE

Mental block, mental image, mental case
All of the above
We're living in a rat's race
Who stole my cheese?
That's not yours!
Big fish, little fish
Pond, lake, stream
Ocean's eleven
A gambler's dream
A play on words
No pun intended
What was the name of that book she recommended?
Idle time, idle thought, idle hand
All of the above
We're moving in an hourglass of sand
What stole my cheese?
No pictures please!

KNOW ME

To know me
Is to understand me
To understand me
Is to like me
To like me
Is to love me
To love me
Is NOT to judge me

GOD BLESS THE CHILD

As a child I had dreams
Although a mother in my teens
As a woman I survived
Not as a statistic, but with pride
To take what life has dealt
No matter how I felt
I had to prove them wrong
To show them I belonged
For I am here to stay
May God bless me along the way

ASSUMPTIONS

Notice me for I am right here
Notice me for I am human
I have qualities
I have needs
I have feelings
I have rights
My heart beats the same as yours
Acknowledge me for I am real
Do you know exactly how I feel
Of course, you don't, had you taken the time
Instead, you chose to read my mind

KILL THEM WITH KINDNESS

Kill them with kindness
That's what I say
One smile goes a long, long way
The more they ignore me
The more I pretend
that they are my very best friend
Kill them with kindness
That's what I say
Don't let miserable people ruin your day

BLAME

Am I the one to blame
Having a chip on my shoulder baring this shame
Trying to fit in with that friendly smile
and they're counting my failures all the while
Stabbed in the back
With gut wrenching pain
Am I to go on as if nothing's changed?
Who pays my bills
Who feeds my hunger pains
Who buys the clothes I wear
Why do I let strangers bother me
It's not as if they care
Are they the ones to blame
Or are they and I one in the same?

CONFIDENCE

Every time I get up you push me down
Have a smile on my face you make me frown
Get one step ahead and you pull me two steps back
It's an ongoing race from beginning to end
Falling to the bottom having to climb up again
Over and over it plays in my mind
I find myself wondering is this a waste of time
Searching for something that seems out of reach
Looking for lessons that life has to teach
True dedication is all that I need
True confidence in myself and I will succeed

THIN LINE

To love; to hate, a thin line between the two
Character and personality, descriptive nouns to describe you
But who are you really?
This I have no clue
Social walls and stereotypes this is a world in which I live
Emotions the coat I put on to keep warm
A smile to mask the winds of political storm
To you I look for the comfort of love
To hate the idea of dependency that thin line I have crossed
Left torn between the two

MIND BLOWING

Mind blowing
Isn't it though?
You mean to tell me that you didn't know?
Who I am and what I represent
For over two hundred years I've been around
With my luscious lips and widely spread hips
My dark chocolate or my creamy caramel complexion
Always gets me some kind of attention
Be it good or be it bad
It's the only life that I've had
I am a black woman and I say it proud
Mind blowing
Isn't it though?
The next time you're asked, you'll already know!

A MOTHER'S LOVE

In the darkest hours of the night
In your arms you held me tight
In my thoughts you were always there
Continuously showing that you care
In tough situations you stood your ground
Explained to me life's ups and downs
A smile you put upon my face
Even when I made the worst mistakes
If I was sick or feeling blue
You always knew just what to do
You raised me well and with respect
A mothers love I'll not forget

DEAR COMFORT ZONE

Don't smile at me and wave your hand
Pretending that you don't understand
Why the hell I feel the way I do
You know damn well it's because of you
I'm tired of you playing all your games
Then acting like I'm the one to blame
I've tried my best to see this through
Now I must forget about you
You're holding me back when I must advance
I'll not miss out on this chance
At war with myself and not finishing
Anything it seems
You still can't take away my dreams

CAGED RAGE

Caged rage
Deep depression
Deep....
Depression
Eludes
Escape
Purposely
Ongoing isolation
The destruction of one's mind
The tears that were left behind
Quietly crying

SOMETHING FOR THE BROTHERS

Hey pretty girl
Do you have the time?
To take a look at a brother like me
One who's not so cute or dresses fly
But has lots of personality
Would I catch your eye?
Or would you pass me by?
Walk'n that walk with your head held high
It's sisters like you that a brother sees through
And you think it's all a game
Sorry, didn't catch your name
Your loss, my gain

MUSIC

Notes create melodies which in turn create songs
As I lie awake listening to the soft sweet sound
Taking me to another level
Mind, body and soul
Peaceful and relaxing yet the motivation is vigorous
Exercising the mind as it flows through me like
A relentless river trying to find its way to the ocean
In tune with the music and in sync with my thoughts
I close my eyes and let myself feel
Feel the rhythm pulsating through my veins
As it makes me tingle all over
This feeling of good
I'm in control, on top of it all
Not a care in the world
I open my eyes realizing that this can't last forever
Just knowing I can return
Makes it all worth the pleasure

TORN LIVES

It seems that no one can understand my need for happiness, my need to be fulfilled
My need for someone to love me
So my needs I keep concealed
I'm torn between two lives, two I need to be as complete
One not letting the other grow, tearing at my soul
The mother in me wanting to nurture
The love in me wanting to be nourished
Holding while being held, loving while being loved
Is that too much to ask?
For happiness, is that such a task?
Don't make me choose between the two
I cannot give up one for the other
I need to be fulfilled as his lover and their mother

FROM A DAUGHTER TO A MOTHER

How do I tell you I love you?
When there aren't enough words to explain
It's automatically assumed
So those words I refrained
We weren't as close as so many
But we both understood it was there
The unbreakable bond that was between us
Actions that told we cared
From a daughter to a mother myself
At times I become overwhelmed
Living my life of expectations
Forgetting about you sometimes it would seem
But just when you needed me I was there
On me you knew you could always lean
I was your back you were my spine
Now it seems that we've run out of time
Looking back I know our love was strong
Those three words were there all along
I LOVE YOU

BROWN EYES

Your brown eyes told me your story of pain
How you've struggled to survive
How you've lived your life in vain
How hard was it to actually maintain?
The movements of your body
The language was all too clear
As you moved with careful steps
So not to show your fear
Hoping maybe that they would disappear?
Your hardened heart and stubborn mind
Has led you so far astray
Never looking back, not wanting
To remember things this way
In all the dreams you've dreamt
None seeming to ever come true
You fall deeper inside yourself
Feeling you were more the fool
And asking how in this life could it be so cruel

INFINITE WISDOM

The power of wisdom comes from the thirst for knowledge and the strength of experience.

Which in turn is life itself

No one can achieve this except you yourself

Although you may falter along the way by getting side tracked and led astray

Eventually things fall back into place and you will continue on at a normal pace

With the experience, knowledge and that

power of...infinite wisdom

FROM ONE SLAVE TO ANOTHER

Softly as the wind whistles by my ear
I knew I had to overcome my fear
To reach my freedom was what I had wanted most
So in the night I fled becoming like a ghost
No more cotton pick'n fields or master's luncheons to prepare
Not many miles to go on from here
Way up north few blacks round there
As the early dawn breaks and I continue on
Oh sweet freedom I'm on my way
I'll own that cotton pick'n field one day

LIFE-LIKE

Like a candle in the wind whose flame burns free
In no certain direction just there, as I remain captivated by its glare
I envy its freedom, its position just to be
Knowing no one will come too close
For fear of being marred, yet being needed at the same time
Until that need is no longer of use
The wind gently blows it out or it flickers a slow death
until the wick has reached the end
Leaving behind few remains that it was even there
Funny how a single candle can resemble life so much

ODE TO THE WORKING MOTHER

To all of the mothers that cook and clean
To all the mothers that run machines
Whether you sit at a desk from nine to five
Whether you're on welfare just trying to survive
Whether you have ten kids or just two
Isn't it time you get what's due
Are you appreciated for all the things that you do
Taking care of the house is a working job too
Although menfolk say you shouldn't get paid
Ask him is he willing to hire a maid

AWARENESS

Moving on keeping strong
Forward in leaps and bounds
Over hurdles through tough times
Still you have survived
Be proud be real
Not ever concealing how you feel
Learning life's lessons
Taking it in stride
Making a turn in the tide
Eyes wide open

PRETENDER

A smile she painted on her pretty face
The sadness she felt they saw not a trace
The glorious life they all thought she had
None of them realizing just how she had it so bad
The struggling pretenses of making things seem
Like she was living her life like a queen
When in reality her dreams were her biggest nightmares
Secretly wondering if anyone cared
If they wanted to know for real how she felt
After all the walls were crumbling and the cards had been dealt
To see if friends would still be around
Or if they'd all just let her down
There's one thing for sure
Keep it real and not for pretend
Lies always catch up
To you in the end

AMONGST OURSELVES

Friend or foe
Foe or friend
In today's America…
Isn't that what it seems?
Black on black crime
Genocide
Light against dark
Lost African pride
Were we not ancestors of African-American slaves
Who died for us
For our lives to be saved
Fought for the rights of equality
Not to be wasted by the economy
They wanted us to believe
In equal opportunity employers
And in God we trust
But what's happened to the rest of us?

HONEY CHILD

Honey child
Don't pay no mind
The shape of your hips, girl you just fine
Honey child
Don't pay no 'tention
That switch in your walk, draws mad attention
Honey child
Don't be ashamed of your skin
That caramel complexion makes tanning a sin
Honey child
Don't you fret
You deserve everything that you get
Honey child
Don't hang your head low
Hold it high so everyone will know
Be proud of who and what you are
A magnificent honey colored child of God

BOTTLED WOMAN.... BLACK?

We bottled things inside
Hiding them for no one else to see
Not knowing we are also hiding them from ourselves
Because we don't even want to see
Looking in the mirror to check
Our make-up, our hair, our clothes
Making sure the image that we portray
Is in tact, so no one knows
How much pain we are in
The scars that have run so deep
The many nightmares we are having
When we are supposed to be asleep
All the damage that was done
While we thought that it was love
We bottled things inside
Instead of praying for help from up above
Blaming ourselves for life's indiscretions,
Those kicks, those punches, those shoves
Whilst holding it together, yeah or so we thought
The bonds of a strong black sisterhood
The life that we were taught
Strong-willed and independent is what they think that we all are
So, we bottled things inside
Like the pickles in a jar
But we are like all other women
Of every culture, every creed
We all have had broken hearts and we all suffer, breathe and bleed

SHE IS

She is patient
She is kind
She is giving of her time
She is special
She is unique
She is a person you'd want to meet
She is someone
She is true
She is bold, brilliant, and beautiful.
She is YOU

PART III: EVOLVE(D)

Evolve(d)
Verb (used with object)
To develop gradually
Verb (used without object)
To come forth gradually into being, develop; undergo evolution
To develop by a process of evolution to a different adaptive state or condition

Women know better than anyone how exhausting it can be trying to find and fight our way through this wilderness called life. Always navigating in the midst of societal woes, and still finding our way to the top.

We are survivors. We are the ultimate chameleons. We adapt to whatever the situation calls for. It's true what they say, "Behind every man is a good, strong woman."

So, let her evolve into the greatness that she is destined for!

To infinity and beyond….

JOURNEY II

Traveling from one place to another.
Passage or progress from one stage to another.
It was in the journey that I became whole
Searching for a destiny
For a peace to sustain my soul
Piece by piece, step by step
A road long traveled
Seemingly without end
Longing for connection amid dysfunction
Traveled upon again and again
Detours...recalculated
Roundabouts...dead ends
Distractions they surround me
Claustrophobia setting in
Many destinations hover
From mountaintops to valleys low
Beckoning to be uncovered…. discovered
Magnified….to be set aglow
My destiny is on the horizon
And I, just need
To look up
Find strength
And GO

LOST AND FOUND

In order to find what is lost
You must lose it to find
Where the sane borders on the insane
That fine line between love and hate
Reality and fantasy
Isn't it all too clear?
The difference between the mind, the heart and the soul
Is the mind separates the logic
The heart intensifies emotion
And the soul verifies the inner strength
That helps keep everything in
Prospective to move on

FINDING LIFE

For in my soul may I find peace
In this so called life in which I lease
As the days, the months and the years have passed
Living each day as if the last
As time came to pass
At life I thought I'd have the last laugh
In the end it played a cruel joke
For in my soul I have found no hope

I SHALL OVERCOME

I shall overcome
My weaknesses, my fears
I shall overcome
As I have through all these years
I shall overcome
As night overcomes the day
I shall overcome
Bringing peaceful silence in a most unusual way
I shall overcome
Strengthening one's awareness, capitalizing on one's mind
I shall overcome
Tyring to get through each moment of this passing time
I shall overcome
Yes! Watch me shall I rise
I shall overcome
As the sun slowly comes up
And takes the night for a surprise

WISH UPON A STAR

Take me here
Take me there
Lord, just take me anywhere
That's not around this stress and strain
Tired of hearing myself complain
Knowing ain't no one else to blame
But carrying on still the same
Hoping I can make a change
In my life to rearrange
My hopes, my dreams, my goals thus far
As I silently wish upon a star

BOOKMARK

As I read through the chapters of my life
The bookmark seems stuck on one page
One paragraph, one sentence, one phrase
The more that I tried to move on
The more I became enraged
Baffled by my inability to proceed
My intuition forced me to read
Clarity then came to my mind
Those pages I then left behind

VISIONS

Look into my eyes, into the windows of my soul
Looks pretty empty and it feels really cold
Loneliness is pretty much my state these days
Looking busy in public but alone in many ways
Ever been in a very crowded room and feel so isolated from everyone at the same time?
I feel like no one can understand me
I'm in a world of my own kind
Being different is kind of cool, it makes me feel unique
Being different also gives me a sense of weakness and defeat
I'm a very sensitive person, whose feelings go really deep
I write down all the thoughts I have before I go to sleep.
Each day I keep telling myself that the next one will be better
Yet every night I go to bed and reread this same letter

PRAYER

I was blinded but you've helped me see
With all the wonderful things you've done for me
I was lost but now I'm found since you've helped
Me stand on solid ground
You made me smile when things looked bleak
Helped me grow stronger when I felt weak
I kneel to you each night I pray
That you'll allow me just one more day
It's up to you, you just say when
I thank you, Lord
Goodnight
Amen

REFORM

I look into the mirror
I take a long hard stare
The image looks familiar but I cannot recognize the face
The reflection is distorted, disfigured somehow
I see no emotions, no reactions
Could it be true what they say?
What you give is what you get in a roundabout way?
For years I've lived in misery, living for someone else
Always people pleasing and not pleasing myself
It's time to take action, regain myself again
Don't worry about those who call themselves my friends.
If I cannot love myself, then who can I love?
Find the purpose in my life and forgive myself, let go
The inner peace will guide me back to the mirror
I will recognize that familiar image, that reflection with emotions and reactions
I'll smile again completely filled with satisfaction.

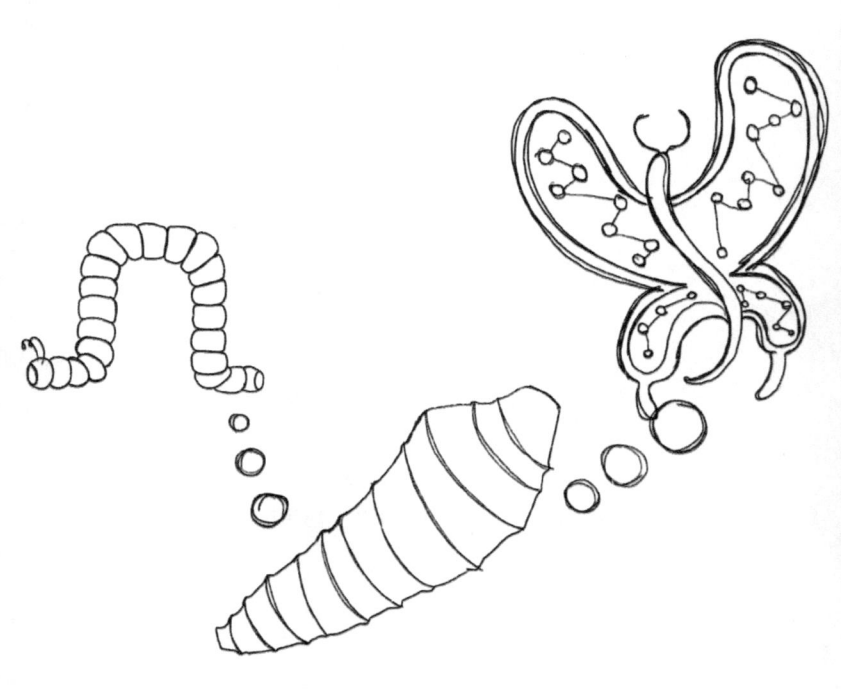

TRANSITION

Like whispering winds and dancing meadows
A peaceful tranquility fills my soul now
Thoughts running over, yet not enough words to describe them
Always wondering if I've done the right thing
The decisions I've made throughout my lifetime
As I sit and look back upon all those younger years
Encouragement could've been a part of it
Strength may have been another
Either way I survived
What's next I'd always say
As if someone knew the answer
And when no answer came it was myself I blamed
Those times are well behind me now
Maturity has set in…now my adulthood begins

REALIZATION

Slowly but surely, I'm coming to grips
Realizing that my life is at my fingertips
The only person who can change my life is me
I need to let go and learn to be free
By putting me first, the knowledge I thirst
The goals that I set, make sure that they're met
Forgiving the past, look toward the future at last
Conquering all fears that have held me for years
Expanding my growth and my spiritual senses
So I can go on and stop building fences
To be and let be, it's all up to me
Everything in life is right nor wrong
It's how we perceive what's going on

LIFE GOES ON

The sun will still shine and the night will still fall
For each has its place in the universe
Still life goes on
Each day we shall rise with wide open eyes
Still life goes on
Through good times and bad
Though we are happy or sad
Still life goes on
Life, it's a never ending cycle
Life is just being
Take time to stop and smell the roses
Enjoy what you have and the dreams you desire
For life can be short
Yet even after you're gone
Still Life Goes On

THE MESSAGE

I look around but I cannot see
Where is the voice that is calling me?
There again!
Can't you hear?
Now it sounds as if it's coming near
Louder and louder, it's calling out strong
Says I should've known Him all along
Come my child, I'll lead the way
Listen to my words heed what I say
For I have come to Bless your soul
To help you reach all of your goals
And in return all that I ask
Is for you to complete one task
Wash away all of your sins
For this is where true life begins
Then join me up at heaven's door
For I know the Lord will have the cure

WHEN WILL IT BE ALRIGHT TO CRY?

When will it be alright to cry?
At your bedside
At your funeral
At the grave site
Or after I clean out your house
Dispose of the things that used to be yours
The things I gave you
The things you saved from long ago
When will it be alright to cry?
When I'm missing you
Or wanting to talk to you just to see how your day went
When will it be alright to cry?
On holidays like Christmas
Your birthday
Mother's Day
When will it be alright to cry?
When I'm supposed to be the strong one
The one you depended on to make sure everything was ok
When will it be alright to cry?
I don't know
I haven't really done it yet
Ruby J Cameron
6-7-1948 to 5-20-2003

RUBY CAMERON

Remembering you will be easy to do
U gave me life
Because I love you
You will always be in my thoughts and dreams
Cause you fulfilled every one it seems
A day won't go by that you aren't missed
Memories won't fade or be dismissed
Even though you're dead and gone
Rest assured you're still loved on
On holidays and regular ones too
Never will we forget about you
Two children… One woman, one man
Left to care for each other the best that they can

FOOD FOR THOUGHT

In a busy and impatient world I found the time to make a way to be still
My thoughts and ideas take me places where I cannot physically go
To far away lands or right next door
But where I want to be, where I need to be
Is right with God

PAST-PRESENT-FUTURE

Yesterday was when I made up my mind
Today is when I finalized my thoughts
Tomorrow is when I will put the actions behind my words and move on away from here
Taking my life to another level
Exceeding all boundaries and expectations
Others have placed before me
In hopes that I would prevail
Hoping that I would fail
Yesterday I would have never dreamed
Today is when my dreams have become conscious efforts
Tomorrow is when they will be a reality to move on away from here
Taking my life to another level
Creating new boundaries and expectations
For others who'll come behind me
In hopes that I will have achieved
All that was destined for me

FINAL DESTINATION

It's been a very long time coming
The time is finally here
A decision must be made
And my mind is so unclear
I've wrestled with this
Resistance mixed with denial
And still I have made no choice
Be still, concentrate, listen to the inner voice
No one wants to be lead on, used or betrayed
I find myself questioning, why I even stayed
It's been a long hard road
Traveling alongside in the shadows of an ego trip
That has long since been played out
I'm exhausted, run down, mentally challenged
Stressed and strained
At times unaware of my surroundings
Where the beginning is and the end stops
Has taken a toll on my soul
It's been a long time coming
And it's time to finally go home

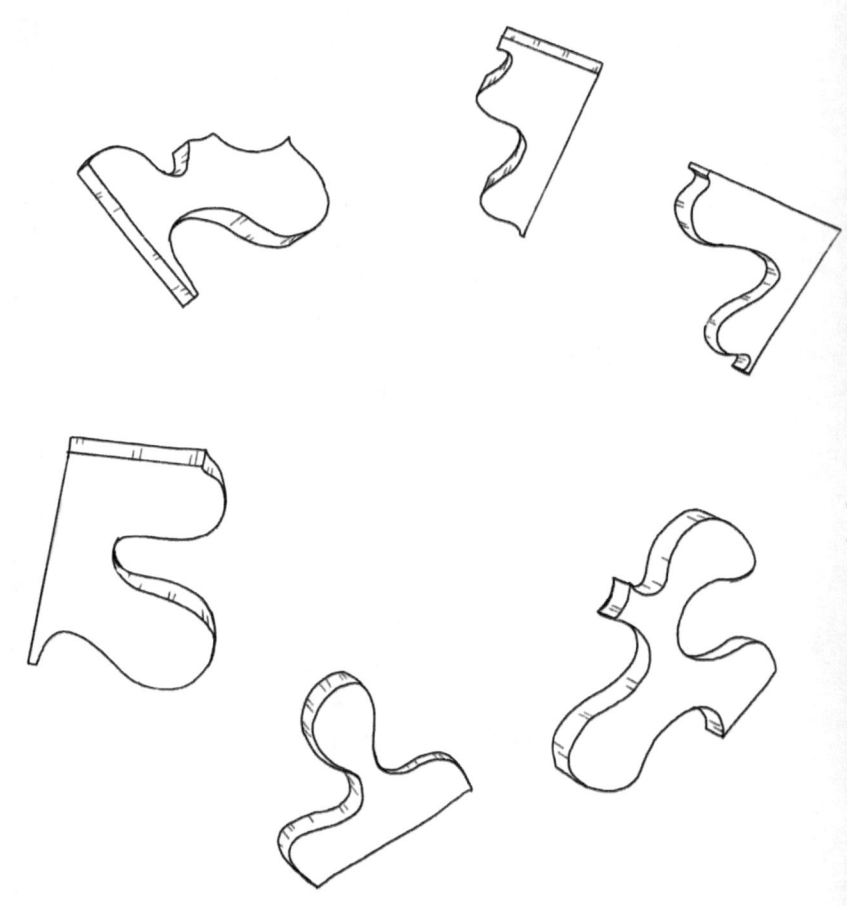

PUZZLE PIECES

My mind's racing in overtime
Always thinking putting things together
A puzzle whose pieces are connecting
I do the edges first those straight lines of life
The middle gets more complicated, more obstacles to endure
As the years go by I pick up the pattern
Just as the puzzle begins to take shape
Things iron out and fill in the blanks
Until I reach the last piece and the picture is clear
And when it is over and the time draws near
In God I have faith and in death no fear

LIFE AFTER DIVORCE

Things have changed
New chapters have begun
A new book perhaps
The other has long been forgotten
Although it is as fresh as a newborn babe
Seems like an eternity has passed me by
I feel old and withered, tired and weak
Life's havoc has taken its toll on me
Left me dried and scorned, depressed and alone
Although there are so many around me
I still search for someone who looks like me
Acts like me, even smells like me
My own reflection is a stranger in my eyes
Being alone has solved nothing
Just made me more aware of what I'm not accomplishing in my life with my time
Time is all I have left and it seems to be running away from me

REST IN PEACE

It was in those fits of anger, those times of rage
Sometimes you'd wish people to their graves
Knowing full well when the moment passed
How you'd wish that stone was not cast
A lot of years have passed between you and I
I know we haven't seen eye to eye
I'd try to give an inch and you'd take a mile
Remembering old times, it makes me smile
Oh my yes, there was a lot of pain but
Occasionally a few rays of sunshine came in through the rain
Do I regret it?
Heavens no!
Everything we went through made me grow
After all these years of putting up with your mess
I never thought of the day that we'd put you to rest
There was a time when you were the love of my life
Our son is nineteen and looks like your twin
And now your true purpose in life begins
All is not forgotten but in my heart I forgave
May peace find you now for the rest of your days
Rest in peace Mr. Robinson

Clifton D Robinson Sr.
9-03-1968 to 4-16-2010

MIND THE DREAM

The mind is constantly in motion
Its wheels turning, thoughts revolving
The would haves
Should haves
Could haves
The won't dos
Might dos
Will dos
All being processed simultaneously
I wouldn't change a thing
Dreaming is the ultimate high creating motivation
Will power
Knowledge
To go through this life in slow motion
Gathering small increments of wisdom at a time
Along the way
It's about not regretting anything
But learning from those past experiences
Teaching yourself and those around you
To put forth an effort into making those dreams come true, don't mind me….
I'm dreaming

BE CONTENT

For all the times I fought and whined
The worldly distractions alive in my mind
When all you wanted for me to do
Was surrender and give my life to you
Chance and luck are what I sought
But providence and power are what you brought
The discontentment I had allowed to push me down
That weakness you used to turn things around
Your amazing grace from lost to found
Your love and mercy put me on solid ground
As joy comes in the morning
Contentment is peaceful rejoicing

GETTING TO HAPPY

Getting to happy
How do you do that?
Is there a step by step guide or some kind of road map?
Every road I've traveled seems to be under construction
detour, right turn, bridge out, clutter, obstruction
Trying to find my way has been no easy feat
Enough of this I'm pulling over and putting God in the driver's seat
I should have known better and I'm glad that I have
Wow riding shotgun ain't too bad
He knows every direction; God's protective system, GPS is rad
Never a detour, wrong turn or destruction
Bridge is always in, organized construction
I've found my guide, my road map, my steps
Allowing God to get me there….
To happy
Has been a journey with no regrets

A TIME 4 ME

It's amazing what I can learn about myself
When I spend time with myself
That sit down
Get still
Be in the moment time
Asking myself questions time
How is my life right now time
Being grateful
Enjoying my Blessings
Worshipping, praising
Just saying thank you time
Not monitoring your time
But minding my time
I love my time
Not wasting my time
Energy or mentality on trying
To make YOU fit into it time

MY BROTHERS KEEPER

You are my brother; you are His son
And after thirty short years
Now I am the only one
Our mother who gave birth to just us two
To be preceded in death by the both of you
With a feeling of pain left for loves residue
I look to the clouds
I ask why; how is this to be
In the stillness I'm told
To keep you close to me
For I dare not to question His purpose or His reason
All that I'm told is
It is time for a new season
It will be through my faith that I will come to understand
That when the time is right
He will reveal to me His plan
I'll know that He's got me in the palm of His hand
In truth our lives are nothing but a line in the sand
It was through God's grace Edward…
My brother, lived long enough to become a man
For He is my brothers keeper

Edward James Cameron
"E"
1-19-1985 to 9-7-2015

WOMAN

The woman I am
The woman you see
You ask how this came to be
The knowledge
The integrity
The independence it took
I could never retrieve from the pages of any book
The hard work
The sweat
The goals that were set
Each day determined to make sure they were met
The mothering
The caring
The house cleaning I've done
A slave of necessity I'd then overcome
To express my ideas
To learn from mistakes
Is this why you think that I am so great?
No the woman I am
The woman you see
Just has the intelligence in this life to be me

UNTIL TODAY

Until today
I had my fears through attitudes and tears
Until today
I've told lies to comfort my absent tries
Until today
I would not trust, living life with anguish and disgust
Until today
I did not live, unable of myself to give
Until today
They ask me why?
With a smile I reply
Until today
I was not whole, I've found the place they call the SOUL

REST ASSURED

I never really imagined my life without you
I felt like you'd be around forever
Although I know we must all say good-bye sometime
I just never thought it would be so soon
I didn't get a chance to say I love you one last time
Although I was right there at your side
Maybe it was pride but from the look in your eyes
I could tell that you knew how I felt
It gives me some peace to know that you waited
Waited for my return out of your concern for me
You waited for me to be by your side
When you drew you last breath you looked so peaceful and free
I love you for teaching me to be me
My strength, my pride, my spirituality, my knowledge, my self worth are all from you
We'll see each other again I'm sure
And when that time comes
When I see you again
I won't hesitate to say I love you
No matter if you know it or not
I miss you mommy and I love you a lot

DREAM

D is for deserving everything that life has to offer
R is for realizing the choice is yours to be made
E is for evaluating your options and moving forward
A is for admitting your mistakes and then doing better
M is for making things happen, not letting them happen to you

DREAM

Thank you for sharing this poetic journey with me. Possibly a journey you've been on yourself. I'm sure many women can relate. It doesn't stop here, we are always learning, growing and evolving. Just as life keeps propelling forward so must we!

Turning dreams into realities…Uprising
"The desire accomplished is sweet to the soul." -Proverbs 13:19
KJV

Poetically Yours,
Tasha Cameron

SUCCESS

S is for the seed that was already planted
U is for the understanding and not taking things for granted
C is for the courage it took for you to even try
C is for the consistency that helped you make it by
E is for the effort that's finally paying off
S is for the struggle but you maintained
when everyone else thought you were at a loss
S is for the success for which you now have achieved
For sticking to your dreams when no one else would believe
Success is in the eyes of its beholder
Whatever you make of it…it shall be yours

ACKNOWLEDGEMENTS

To my sons, Clifton Robinson Jr. and Tyquan Cooper, who had more faith in me than I initially had in myself.

To Maggie Dean who typed and retyped my manuscript helping me ascend to this momentous occasion.

To Calvin Keith Rose II for his artwork – bringing my ideas into a visual completion.

ABOVE ALL …

This glory belongs to God, because without His gift and purpose I would not have become.

⁶ Being confident of this very thing, that he who hath begun a good work in you will perform it until the day of Jesus Christ.

-Philippians 1:6 (KJV)

www.ingramcontent.com/pod-product-compliance
Lightning Source LLC
Chambersburg PA
CBHW020911080526
44589CB00011B/543